Quantum Leap

Janice Powell

Quantum Leap © 2022 Janice Powell

All rights reserved.

No part of this publication may be reproduced, stored in a retrieval system, or transmitted, in any form or by any means, electronic, mechanical, photocopying, recording or otherwise, without the prior written permission of the presenters.

Janice Powell asserts the moral right to be identified as author of this work.

Presentation by *BookLeaf Publishing*

Web: www.bookleafpub.com

E-mail: info@bookleafpub.com

ISBN: 9789357610971

First edition 2022

DEDICATION

For the one in my life with the smile that stands out.

PREFACE

Is it possible to truly understand love if one has never had true love with another? I often ask myself if my love is love when I love someone. I do this because no one has ever loved me in return. I contemplate all of this and in the end, each time I come to the conclusion that my love is real and valid. I understand love because I was born with a passion for it and the desire to help others on their journeys with it. The poems in this book describe the feelings that come from my experience with love. Many focus on the harsh reality of unrequited love, while some of the others describe the focus and calm love gives us. A main topic within the poems is the power of what exists behind the surface of that smile one comes across that is different from the rest. These poems are not elaborately edited because I value keeping them as close as I can to what comes from my heart.

Dawn

On the day we meet
Come and take a walk with me
Through the newborn trees
That left us a grassy tunnel
Between them

Every morning
Come and take a walk with me
Until our walks fade the grass away
As the trees seem to snuggle closer
Each new day
Let our love continue to keep that grass away

Come and take a walk with me
When our wrinkles are dense
Like parched cracked desert land
And our hair is completely white
Like new untouched snow
Hold my hand
With your silk soft one
Now softer than it was
When we met fifty years ago
As we cut the ribbon
To make it official
The naming of our highway

Come and take a walk with me
When we have moved in with the wind
Where the frigid cold can't touch us
We can stir the leaves our tunnel trees
Left us to dance in
Until they help us take shape again
And then
In the thick fog
Kiss me before rush hour begins

Northern Lights

Little sense it makes
This I know
But I fell in love with her
Without meeting her face to face
To meet her lips
Mattered little
Compared to matters of her heart
Her values are pure diamonds and gold
Shimmering in her smile
Like the sun glimmers on a lake
Glancing into its water
I look for my reflection
But hers took its place
All that matters
Is how her soul
Fills my space
She engulfs me from far away
Years and years pass by
And still
Everyday after I wake
As the day goes by
I relive moments of heartbreak
I keep her put away in my soul
I have to keep her in my safe
Never opening it for long
So I can stay sane

Awake

I never knew what peace looks like
Until I saw her smile
I have never seen a smile like hers
Her smile is awake
Without coffee
It is as if every other smile
Was asleep
Sleepwalking through life
Her smile endures
She has x-ray vision
To see the good within the hard

Dream Girl

My favorite moments are
The nights you meet me
In my dreams
It is the only place I can see you
You visit me often
In this alternate reality
I will never forget the night when you kissed me
What does it mean
When I have not even met you in person
One time would mean very little
A rambling of the mind
But you return again and again
Like a life-changing quote
And in there, you are mine
It seems the best and strongest
Connections do not need bodies
Sleep was once just an escape
From reality and anxiety
Now it is the way to see my dream
Girl walking beside me
As clear and vivid as if I am awake
Like it is virtual reality
I hope it means
You will be in my arms one day
When I am awake

And nothing is fake
For my heart's sake
I love you, my dream girl
I love your mind
How everything you believe is behind
The window in your smile
Your smile has become my map
To the place I want to reside
It is where my dreams come true
Where I have you
Where pain subsides
Where my potential does not hide
You make dreaming urgent and easy inside
You changed the tide
I am not drowning anymore
My feet found the ocean floor
I could finally walk to shore
Now, every wave, I ride
I do not look down
I look ahead
I fly

Tied

I think love
Does not form from memories
When I met you
I already knew you
I recognized your soul
I know we will find each other
In future lifetimes
So I did not
Come to love you
From what transpired in this one
I already began loving you
Before you arrived
I have been loving you
Since the dawn of time
But time is an illusion
The many versions of love we share
Exist all at once
None are better than any
They are all tied

Antidote

Her eyes inject me with dye
To find the poison
That seeks to kill my poise
Her heartbeat is my white noise
Her smile points out how I am chosen
Just like her
To send waves of healing
To the broken

New Age

Many live many years as widows
The departed went early to the next lifetimes
We should not dismiss
The much younger ones that love us
They already suffered so long without us
In their last lives

Fountain Coin

I don't hate myself
I still want to be me
But I hate that it doesn't interest her
It's like this lifetime is karma
I've been created this way
So she would not want me
It must be a punishment
For failing her in another life
I'm a coin
In a fountain
Flipped as heads
She can't see tails underneath
Where I know she is perfect for me
She won't go in for me
Nobody does that at a fountain
She only glanced my way
Barely noticed me
I'm a coin
In a fountain
With a glitch
Worth a lot
The reflections through the water
Hide it
The coins all around me

Disguise it
Through the water
I see her with a woman
That doesn't know the treasure she has
But I say nothing
I'm immobile and mute as a coin
I love her quietly

Leaps

Her smile sends me on quantum leaps
I always arrive where I needed to go
She does this when I have yet to meet her
Who could blame me for loving her
Anyone experiencing the same would too
She gives so much from afar
Imagine how much more it would be
Standing next to her
I want to ride the leaps
To my dreams
I want to send her on leaps too
I need to give back
The enormous gifts she has given me

Gift of Love

My love for you
Is spilling over into my lungs
I feel like I am drowning
I want to drain it
Turn it to ink
Write you letters with it
Perhaps I will
But I won't mail them

Because your heart
Was not able to care
When I spilled my feelings before
I sit here now
Knowing that when I'm near the end
One day
There will be boxes and boxes of letters
I had to write to you
To keep my lungs free
Because you weren't able to love me

[I imagine wrapping them for Christmas
Putting them under our tree
To show you how I held onto you
So many years
Before you finally chose me]

Underwater

I need you to find me, my love
My heart is holding my breath
Let's say my lifespan is
The amount of time I am able
To hold my breath underwater
I feel like I'm nearly out of air
I need you to find me, my love

Locked Out

All the pain I have suffered
It was clues
Your smile is the treasure
Layered, solid, not hollow
But you are surrounded
By security
I can only look at you from a distance
Every time I do
I learn something new
I just wish I knew
The password to you

Love on Steroids

You were born on the day of love
No sliver of surprise there
Love is your gift
Love is your creed
Your message is the world's need
Your words are the seed
For growth
You invade my heart
Like a vine weed
Weaving in every direction
To remove you
Would destroy me indeed

Legacy

I wish the words I need
From my heart
Would be delivered to me
The same way they stream
So easily
When I change to my channel
Of silent peace
And connect with the universal energy
Words are the only way to her
They're the path beyond
What she sees of me physically
More than any bestseller
I just want to write
A letter
A poem
A book
Anything
That draws her to me
I hope writing is my gift for this very deed
For my love for her is my legacy

The Mystery

Her smile is my sunrise
Her safety is my sunset
I was made to love her
So why am I without her
It's the one thing I will never get

Locked In

When I see her smile
I know that she knows
The way to feel alive
She knows the way
To paradise of the mind
My mind has felt like constant winter
For as long as I can remember
Her smile changed the season
The way I reason
Now I'm locked in for life

Fortress

If you read my mind
You will know where you take me
Castles in snow storms

Soliloquy

Smiles were just paintings
Before I saw yours
Your smile is a painting, poem, play, song...
All forms of art at once
As your lips curve into it
It is the the curtains opening
From there I watch our forever together
Flash before my eyes
I am immersed so deeply
I forget I am not by your side

www.ingramcontent.com/pod-product-compliance
Lightning Source LLC
LaVergne TN
LVHW021351200726
843509LV00014B/2799